EARLE STREET

EARLE STREET

poems

ARLEEN PARÉ

Talonbooks

Talonbooks
9259 Shaughnessy Street, Vancouver, British Columbia, Canada V6P 6R4
talonbooks.com

Talonbooks is located on xʷməθkʷəy̓əm, Sḵwx̱wú7mesh, and səlilwətaʔɬ Lands.

First printing: 2020

Typeset in Arno
Printed and bound in Canada on 100% post-consumer recycled paper

Interior design, cover design, and cover illustrations by andrea bennett

Talonbooks acknowledges the financial support of the Canada Council for the Arts, the Government of Canada through the Canada Book Fund, and the Province of British Columbia through the British Columbia Arts Council and the Book Publishing Tax Credit.

LIBRARY AND ARCHIVES CANADA CATALOGUING IN PUBLICATION

Title: Earle Street / Arleen Paré.
Names: Paré, Arleen, 1946– author.
Description: Poems.
Identifiers: Canadiana 20190140941 | ISBN 9781772012507 (SOFTCOVER)
Classification: LCC PS8631.A7425 E27 2019 | DDC C811/.6—dc23

For my neighbours, who are friendly and kind

all night the house felt like it was underwater
red gills beneath each shingle opening and closing
to receive the air

—Don Domanski
All Our Wonder Unavenged (2007)

CONTENTS

This Street Is a Window

This Street Is a World

This Street Is a River

STREET LIFE

                      is windowed   angled right   rect cornered and lined
lineated and justified left   wooden and glass   is panels of light   light rain and
heavy   frames with leaves in a hurry   outside orientations   landscape portrait
the green of the foliage coined quartered seen through six horizontals of old
mullioned glass in their hundreds their millions quaking always shaking in
the multifaceted wind   sudden pieces of sky   blue horizontal   pieces of bark
scored   the peace of the morning pierced with robin sound   sure-pitched
predictable notes   that clarity   purpose   the way the jade joy   those leaves
almost round   fits into these straight upright shapes   the window allowing
fitting it in   these intimacies   the street at the right distance   far enough off
and almost safe

KEY-SHAPED, THE SHADOW

To render a portrait, a likeness, you must begin with the small key-shaped
cast-shadow under the nose. In the same way, to render a street, a room. To
render a window, start with the pane. To build a house, start from the centre
of the second-floor bedroom. Out to the drywall painted peanut-shell beige. If
assembling a car, a charcoal Corolla, start from the plush of the Corolla's back
seat. Or constructing a street from under the street, from inside the sewers,
temperamental tunnels with insufficient diameter, catch basins, clay tiles,
storm drains, whatever is unspeakable: start there. Whatever rises then to the
top, to manhole covers, inside and out, spreading topographical over the
pavement, over the edges where lawns fringe the sidewalks. Start from the
inside, as though organic, as though building from inside a seed.

CITY TREES

As for these ruffled pillars,
these rough steadfast organics festooning the boulevard,
risking cement and poisonous fumes, separated
one from another by stretches of grass,
parked cars, tarmac, wires, and walls.
As for the Japanese katsura, the European hornbeam
the willow, weeping alone in the park,
as for the linden viburnum, yellow cedar,
the Italian prune plum, horse chestnut,
as for the bigleaf maple, the Japanese cherry,
the apple in the backyard of unknown name.
These ornamental lungs, these inclinations, colour and shape,
singular
or planted in neat urban rows
without comfort of forest or shoulder to cry on,
each one is named harmless, exiled,
named friend.

BLUE MOON ENTERS THE STREET FROM THE SOUTH-EAST

in this chamber I am a goshawk
listening   there are laminations   limitations of
sleep   the casement window
opens out
but not wide

lamentations lift up from night pavement
disembodied   as if small animals   as if
a midnight radio station somewhere
offshore   voices shift   off and on
one pair   then another
a call-in show from Australia
grave opinions   weather systems
a sad book made into a movie
a balloon head on the end of a string
a blue moon at the end of the street
ruminations   the report of a death
someone I'll never know
these sounds doppel by   fading   entering the
ether   the nothing
as if nothing has ever lifted itself into this room
this open window

IN JAPANESE THIS TREE IS *KATSURA*

Katsura, tree of trees, you see me through my bedroom window. Years have you watched, so close I could comb my fingers through your green hair. When I leave, you wait for me to return. Sometimes for days. You are as patient as stone. In the book I am reading, a woman will commit suicide. In some parts of Japan this might be an act of honour. Moral courage, a sense of pride. She will kneel in front of a train. In the book she is simply weary of life. Katsura, your leaves are small lungs. You watch me with so much attention, even when your leaves fall from your branches. Leaving you almost bereft.

dusk bands the sky
barred owl
its own feathered cage

METAPHOR AS METAPHOR

after Michael Erard, metaphor designer

Perhaps a room: the windows and doors frame a view toward what might be real. Say, the outdoors. If you place the windows high up, people will see only branches. Place them low, they see only the trunk.

Sometimes the room can be empty. Sometimes the views from the room can be forced. Perhaps new and therefore uncomfortable. In those situations, you must direct people's attention, you must give them furniture to sit on that makes architectural choices unavoidable. Each of us has our own point of view. A window is not just a metaphor. Nor is a metaphor only a window.

THIS LAND IS A LANGUAGE

how seeing begins with small fragments of knowledge
small frames
before I began to see
I didn't know what I didn't see

gathering here on this page
this street   these rectangulars and irregular verbs
vehicles   curbs   all within these unceded territories
the Songhees and Esquimalt Nations   the Lekwungen and W̱SÁNEĆ Peoples
to acknowledge this
the place where I am

despite discovering that the word
unceded does not appear in the dictionary I use

language does not always keep pace
although it is implicated it is only a part

I pick apples in the backyard   place blue boxes out on the verge
on this *unceded* street
this land does not belong to me
though I now live on this street

the significance historic   linguistic this legal term
where I   where my house   painted medium blue
my life sidewalked and staired rising   descending

even though the word *ceded* appears on page 229
even though *unceded* should follow *unceasing* on page 1577
which should precede *uncelebrated uncensored unceremonious*

at the same time in a parallel universe
the notion of *ceded land*
does not arise in the Coast Salish languages

as if an arm or a foot
could be simply surrendered

EARLE STREET IS A TREE BENEATH
MY BEDROOM WINDOW

Katsura, your leaves are yellow-green hearts that syncopate breezes arising somewhere on the ocean miles to the west. Your foliage, familiar, spreads over the wires, over the street lamp, the utility pole, birds in the front yard, the window, the deer, over voices unseen on the sidewalk, spreads over the garbage truck and the street-cleaning truck and the cars that belong to the parents or grandparents of the children who arrive at the daycare across. Your leaves hinder the view. In the summer, I can stand naked at the upper-floor window. Unseen. Forest bathing. Your two-sided leaves screen the scene inside and out.

this rain forest
no rain
for weeks

A BRIEF HISTORY OF THE MODERN CITY

a found poem

in the beginning a city is no broader
than can be crossed in an hour on foot

standards   intersections   narrow windows and oil-burning lamps

in the beginning Peking Damascus and Rome
so many people   years   revolutions
peasant political ecclesiastical industrial sweeps

more change than anyone could cross
in a morning

in 1815 Baron Haussmann tore down
the old Paris slums   those jumbles
sewers open to sky

the language of roads enters the mind
the lexicon
Paris so handsome
not even the Nazis could bear to burn it to ground

smooth streets and ample   main roads set at right angles
and though Jane Jacobs claims that no direct relationship can be found
between morals and housing
urban grid patterning uncomplicates thinking

finding your way   and the car
can cross neighbourhoods in less than an hour

straight-sided houses   convenient measures
not that streets are simply political
who's allowed to walk in what parts of a city but
I have to ask –
those Paris slums

                  where are all those people

THRESHOLD

the neighbour who walks her west highland white averts her morning gaze
and the man who approaches his old tercel who always asks which one of us is
which   sisters or twins   he now turns his back   as does the old man who sits
in his black stacking chair on his stoop

even this short goodbye kiss   not outside but not inside the house either   at
the basement door partially open   a commonplace ritual   bye dear   stay safe
have a good one   is now unsettling at the threshold between one woman and
another

the two-by-two children who cross the street parkwise singing at a long
forty-five-degree angle   *row row row your boat*   the children pay us no
mind at all

THIS STREET IS / IS NOT A RIVER

this street is a strategy   an abode biding time
warp and weft   east to west   or perhaps walking on the diagonal
buying sockeye on sale at the mall
a half-block away   galvanized
nails   nail brushes from the Home Hardware
drugs at the Heart
this street is a convenience   double-edged
a place for the impermanent
and for those who never leave

welcome to the cult capital
wizards and covens
said the ferry terminal cashier
that first day we moved to Vancouver Island

beyond conventions of home   homeyness
hi honey homonyms   ad hominems
almost homogenous   *heigh-ho heigh-ho*

my father's father in County Antrim born out of wedlock
raised with the horses and sheep

a rivulet runs under   a watercourse unlit by sky
a ruined Garry oak meadow minus the camas minus
chocolate lilies   pink shooting stars   bright yellow tips
that kind of damage   progress   the underside of

ও

when I first moved here twelve years ago the street was a siding
a way station between worlds   a small human procession
moving at the rate of blood circulating around the human knee
back then everyone who walked past me
had a face in skin tones of grey
they wore hell's horns on their well-salted heads
a never-never land in isolation

i don't know
maybe the street chose us
two sidewalks running parallel lines   a kind of safety
not quite solace   an island inside an island

my mother's father   his office job at the Northern Electric
heart bursting there   six children at home

the inside-outness of this vantage point
this particular place on the globe   a mild foreboding
this bedroom window   second-floor
its own solitary dimension
who's not an outsider
its own half-light   a form of void

࿔

the house is a boat   floats
some outsiders are more outside
whoever abides here with me on this block
on this two-way tar-track with no life-saving bumps
keeps their true thoughts inside their breast pockets

wires caught like fishing line in the katsura
the overstorey of boulevard trees

cars shortcut the major arterial route
heedless of the Hollywood Park located midway
a pseudo la la land that hooks onto the main thoroughfare
which heads off
toward the blue-bounded sea

࿔

this street is not four storeys high   not layered   not wedding cakes
or Black Forest or *Tales of Hoffmann*   though the Offenbachs
live five houses down and across

red arches at their feng shui door   where last month
suddenly the mother died
and last year the sister
the father still makes small wooden soldiers
leafing gold flakes onto their tiny lapels

this street is not a Hollywood movie
despite the eponymous park   not *The Sound of Music*
not a book   not *Jane Eyre* or "The Wasteland"   not exactly
although it harbours shadows and hedges   half moons
the mildewy leaves of red roses
broken devices   broken glass

also nightmares and the occasional thief
a drum kit   an old sewer system   storm drains
a family of deer that eat stargazer lilies but leave lavender
untouched
English and French   Spanish as well

twin babies cry   mothers cry
and while none of these homes are constructed of glass
so much is frangible

my family will not leave me alone
nor do I leave them unattended

this street offers no safe needle-disposal sites
no steel yellow boxes affixed to utility poles
no old school *flâneurs* wander by in dark-blue berets

&

this street is not a flood of new ideas
not treeless   nor full open to sky
not tolerant or intolerant altogether
not lacking in song-specific buff-coloured birds
or song-deprived crows   not without its fixed
delusional degenerate in wraparound shades
worn even in rain

it is not without a daycare or optometrist
or amateur car mechanics bookending the corners at the midwest
not without baseball fields or an empty house
so far unhaunted   or not

I can no longer listen to the world's unravelling
plastic bags at the shoreline   cars   leaf-blowing machines
I am overcome by the fumes

my family visits without calling ahead   even at night

the street lamps do not illuminate the edges of ordinary dread
pitch-dark   street light gets lost in the branches
which every night scratch at my single-pane glass

ॐ

this street is afloat in precision and time
on a wetland of history   a nano-flash
you could sink to your knees
it goes nowhere   but to the heart
still breathing   a small *boketto*   a gaze from the portals
starship midway to nothing much

it is not a haven   no one owns a blue backyard pool
nor are there vegetables in every garden
nor a chicken in every pot   nor a ham

ॐ

across the street   a stay-at-home mum
her children grown up almost gone
polishes the silver
hood of the family's new pickup truck
phones us when a tree topples in overnight wind
she watches for cars that don't belong
for lost dogs   noxious weeds   oiled water pooling at curbside
noises   small fissures in the street's presentation

while the sound of the underground river
while native grasses attempt restoration   interrupt
thoughts of my mother in her green suede high heels

I don't mention
belonging   being here only twelve years
uncertain how neighbours perceive
the missing husband   children too
the way we hold ourselves   she and I   like hinged gates

two other women move onto the street
they own two black-and-white dogs
erect an orange cat in the living room window

this street is not a pipeline and yet there is gossip
it is not a river   and yet a river

under the drain in our basement near the back door
the floor is webbed and cracked   the water table rising
puddles   clumps of wet rotten root

eyeball pressed to the small concave grate   water rushing
mouth to the bars   blind trout with eyes bulging like marbles
the water shines black
the river sings under the iron disc of a grill
perpetual risk

all houses on this street
rest on the flow inside their pale stucco crusts
I say this to no one: on this street
when the earthquake subducts   there will be
liquefaction

above all   this place is my eco-environment
my now geo-niche   my backyard and front
my almost home
extension of self   ecosystem   my forest   meadow
my immediate surround
this street is what happens in the morning
when I open the blinds

the orange cat grows large behind its glass pane
spiders web the back windows where winds blow them like sails
trees mature
whenever a truck rumbles the road
the bed pulses and shakes

SMOKE

time of year   incoming weather   according to nobody's plan
random mistakes
matches   predictions   wildfires in the heartland
houses and horses   evacuations from small bc towns
canaries and dogs
hundreds   thousands of hectares   pine trees
and owls in the trees

no rain on the coast in this rainforest landscape
for weeks
some version of paradise   ocean sunsets
and yet
this unholy fog
smoke dense enough to irritate eyes
its provenance   five or eight hundred miles to the
east where the fires where easterly winds
now drift over the strait
smoke you can lift off car windshields
shirt collars   shoes
particles   white ash
you can wipe from the surface
of stiff curling leaves

This Street Is an Arboretum

Not that I want to be a god or a hero.
Just to change into a tree, grow for ages, not hurt anyone.

—Czesław Miłosz
"Notes," in *Bells in Winter* (1978)

BEFORE STREETS, THERE WERE STREETS

Before glaciers, before
glaciers receded, before art on the walls of Chauvet,
pyramids, long before that,
days lay end to end, flat,
canopies of light,
conundrums of vines, wetlands, deserts.
Night always in mind.

Before sundials, before clocks tick-tocked light to dark,
before latitude, longitude, cement, before steel,
girders, before windows spanned rooms,
spawned views, millennia before grid patterning,
before all that:
      the Pole Star, Southern Cross,
rivers, tracks, ridges,
migrations, leading,
following following
winds, katabatic, prevailing,
ocean currents:
all forms of streets
before streets.

WHAT COUNTS FOR JUSTICE IN POSTMODERN TIMES

It's not that I don't value the street, its numbered logic, lineation. Nor do I dislike its name. No. It's that I love you more, Katsura. Your rough texture, your heartwood, your valentine leaves the size of a child's open palm. Layered, multitudinous, thin bells on bells. Rooted so lightly in soil. In Beirut, there is an absence of street numbers, street signs. My friend's house can be found by narrative alone: *the house on the road with the red-roofed café across from the shop with the faded blue door*. In some seasons, the blue door is ajar or somewhat obscured. Some friends never arrive. In Freetown, too, where my sister once lived, men and women hold hands without hands, sit without feet on streets without names. What heartwood covers the heart: all this placed side by side on the page. In summer, Katsura, your foliage hides the street outside our yellow door.

grey squirrel
races the fenceline
no one wins

COME THE UNGULATE

come the ungulate   through the streets   the gates   come the deer   they
will   on sidewalks   small groupings   come the doe and the fawn   families
come the buck   through the streets as if there were none   they will   com-
plicate   five or six   they thread through   across   ignoring the cross   they
will   intersections   three fawns behind   they will on the diagonal   stop signs
or stoplights   come the deer   they will at their own   laneways and boule-
vards   ungulate   they will regal   their pace   they will slow   through cars
they will   from the north   they come   problemate   laneways   they will
roads   into backyards   front yards   they will graveyards   in the southern
direction   as if   preferring the young tops of short trees   miniatures   pear
trees and cherry   they will   over fences   arrive   come the roses   prefer
they will yellow and red   recline   the cemetery is two hundred years old
they will   overlooking the ocean   range   until the ocean   lie down   as
if no one   lounge between headstones   they are not ready to die   three
buck   they will ruminate   consume   come the deer   out of campuses and
government gardens   come the deer   come the people   the love   come
the hate   under street lamps   weave   come the park   they will bend their
dark-shadowed necks under spliced overhead light   three deer on the grass
flower beds and hedges   antlers   charcoal grey   navy blue   they will   they
could be three oversized hounds   under the broken beam   stillness below
the 3 a.m.   the window   they will   paying no attention   as if no human
population   no houses   they will   their place   come the doe   buck   come
the fawn   come cougar   hunger   come evening   the night

CLOSE NEIGHBOURS

Somebody said somebody poisoned somebody's dog.
Across the street. In their backyard.
Thirteen years ago. Maybe more.
The dog barked all day.
Sometimes at night.
They were across-the-fence neighbours on the north side,
white picket, and also the dog had dug up the petunias.

Those two houses, side by side in urban proximity.
No one had proof.
The owners both moved away. Both
houses are still painted white, clapboard,
and the roofs are both charcoal gray.

The dog was found in the morning,
a terrier, they said, not breathing or even twitching,
its back stiff against the white picket fence.

THE BLOCK WATCH CO-CAPTAIN
EMAILS REGARDING MORE B AND E'S

a found poem

the police would like to remind you to keep your eyes and ears open for persons
suspicious or vehicles   beaters or hummers   moving trucks   flatbeds in your
neighbourhood   skateboards persons not wearing seasonal clothing or wear-
ing sunglasses in inclement weather   there have been residential B and Es in
the area between five and six in the morning   suspects are targeting homes
with no activity   police encourage you to keep   locked and secure   report
suspicious activities   fires set on the curbside   wearing masks   if you plan
to leave   vacation or business   here are some tips   have a friend stay in your
home   or many friends   lock your doors   ask a friend to come by   make
many friends   put newspaper and mail deliveries on hold   or picked up by
a friend   right away   lock your doors   lock your windows   have a friend
one of many   use an alarm   keep your eyes and your ears   report flatbeds
hummers   fires on curbsides   early-morning human activity with or without
balaclavas and masks

THEY KNOW YOUR FACE

crows everywhere are everyday common
their gothic glut
their noise piercing mammalian sleep   their claws   strut
their own particular laws
the street rendered murderous
pugnacious barons robbers in black satin coats
loosening the day's simple seams   they
gather gutter lord
lord and mutter   rampage
sour the clouds with uncommon complaint

fish head and rabbit's foot   a half ham and cheddar on rye
crows swallow all   living and dead   certain shades
red   belly-up on the road   rags   rotted teeth

sidewalk toddlers   flocks of
are targets   also hair   hats   songbirds   small trucks
eagles   cats   take-home sushi in styrofoam boxes

whatever moves   all things unmoving too   they
they know your heart
by heart   your thin nose   your
oversized chin   how you hunch
when you run for the bus in the rain

URBAN GEOGRAPHY I

a found poem

the increasingly sociological and anthropological perspective of inquiry
privileges the anonymous and the everyday in which zoom lenses cut out
metonymic details   parts taken for whole   slowly   representatives that
formerly symbolized families groups   orders   disappear from the stage that
they dominated during the epoch of name   we witness the advent of number
it comes with the system   democracy   large cities   administrations   cyber-
netics   a flexible and continuous mass woven tight as a fabric with neither
rips nor mended patches   a multitude of quantified heroes who lose names
and faces as they become the ciphered river of streets   a mobile language of
computations   rationalities   belonging to none

URBAN GEOGRAPHY II

a found poem

Spaces and places should not be closed but be open   crosscut   some from
within   some from without   made up of belonging   but whose belonging
should take priority   resulting in the dominance and resistance of spatialized
practice   underdetermined by existing structures   spatial of course   openings
new forms   the performance   a form of hand in hand   mutable and
clearly unfixed

Moreover the notion that the performer for instance the social agent and the
contest of performance for instance the space or the place are distinct from
one another should be abandoned   both are entangled in the heterogeneous
processes of spatial becoming

How to find out what's going on on the street   which social agent's small baby
cried through the night   for instance   or their dog barking undeterred by
existing strictures clearly unfixed entangled in spatial unbecoming without
comfort or rest

AN EMAIL REGARDING A SUSPICIOUS EVENT

a found poem

I could hear him   my window was open   I tiptoed to the living room   my
other motion light clicked on and there he was on a cellphone walking away
then back again   he saw me   he walked back onto my lawn close to my
tenant's closed window

what are you doing my neighbour shouted   and the guy left

I phoned the police   they came but they didn't catch him   the motion lights
didn't stop him   mid-twenties black jacket blue jeans on a cell   empty beer
can near the window this morning   my cup of coffee on the kitchen table   in
a new light

COME THE CROWS

come the crows come the crows come
their song   as if
come their nests   come
their families friends bullies bosses
come their want
come their dangerous beaks
their inscrutable eyes
mornings   their pluck
come their unstinting drive
how many stones
were ever needed
their resolve
the crows
uninvited
evermore
evermore

URBAN DEVELOPMENT

reconstruction implies
destruction first

to raise implies
to have razed

too many new buildings
too much new cement

not that all streets must be political
posters   soapboxes   hammers and tongs

who has even seen
a soapbox this century

but tell me again   what happens
to those who are driven out

A MISCHIEF OF RATS – OR A PLAGUE

rats would be almost agreeable
if they weren't so
multiplicitous   determined   so nighttime   so
gnawing straight through cement mortar tin cans
rubber hoses PVC piping brick walls plaster and lathe

what then could keep them from gnawing
straight through your baby's soft cheek

and yet   despite their overlong tails
that end in a point
despite their skitter across bedroom floors
their conical snouts
their collapsible skulls
their ruby black eyes
their oversized laser-sharp teeth
rats might be almost   somewhat
agreeable

SMALL RAT

Bless the dead rat
on its side in the grass
facing the wall.
Just that one rat.
Alone. Starved maybe
or struck in the street some hour of night
making for the neighbour's backyard,
too fast or too slow. Or poisoned.
Or maybe it was life in the storm drains,
tenuous, tense, the young rat finally
just giving up.

URBAN GEOGRAPHY III

a found poem

urban geography   universities   the anglo world   second world war
not included as a separate topic in the same way that geomorphology or
climatology or indeed political and economic geography   prior to that   this is
understandable in relation to the city it tended to concentrate on consequence
towns being descriptive   this is the most popular   when readers ask for cities
or towns or poetics   the issue of description   the issue of what is concrete
gives cities a colossal head start   concrete is what cities do best

THE QUESTION OF DELIGHT IN THE MAELSTROM OF THE SORROWING WORLD

What chimera of yellow birds in flight could be more dizzying? These leaves that remain, small discs of sunlight. The wind blows and they shiver, shine. What about vertigo? The risk. The world in spill upside down, unbalanced, reeling, as leaves peel off one by one. As we lean on the unstable air. We depend on our ears, on language to make life surpass what it will become, as we depend on failing leaves to shimmer with or without any sun. What about thrall, kaleidoscopic? Small garments slipped. Limbs undressed, turn into roots exposed to the cold.

late autumn rain
the cup
still overspills

AND ADAM NAMED EVERY STREET

Earle Street after Thomas Earle,
grocer, wholesaler, pioneer, B.C. MP.
Blanshard Street after Richard Blanshard,
barrister, governor.
Douglas Street after Sir James,
fur trader, governor, Hudson's Bay factor.
Yates after James Yates,
builder, saloons, MP. St. Charles Street
after a saint.

Fort Street after a fort.
Store Street after a store.
Linden after a tree.
Faithful Street, a virtue.
Government, after an old institution.

Foul Bay Road after a bay that would not hold Captain Vancouver's anchor.

That kind of prerogative. Pre-emptive. Foundational.

Milton, Chaucer, Byron, all names of streets in this city.
Wordsworth, Browning, Shelley, Shakespeare, and Keats.

One street called Quamichan, of the Coast Salish Peoples.
One street named Pandora, the woman who opened the box.

INSIDE OUT

Mid-week sun on the grass when the paramedics
load him into the van, the old man
who rents the house across the street and one down.
Who knows that old man?

Before this, did he sleep through the night?
Did he eat fish? White fish or red? Red wine or white?
Lettuce from neighbourhood beds?

The grocery store banned him six months ago. That much we know.
Everyone knows that much about the old man.
His lascivious letters to the women who work in the deli. And to women
who live on the street.
Letters, three pages long, in their mailboxes.
We know about that.
We know to watch out as he scuttles at angles,
human crab crossing the street. We know his furtive
peaked cap and long coat in the cold. And yet
who knows what year his wife died?

Does he see us now peering through our front window
as he struggles to sit up on the stretcher
laid out on his lawn
waiting
for the paramedics to take him away.
Banned from drugstore and bank.

Did he listen to talk shows? Did he write to the Pope?
Did he use pencil or pen?

NIECE I: WE LONG FOR OURSELVES
EVEN AS WE SLIP AWAY

Katsura, you leave yourself everywhere this time of year, nonchalant, unpinning your stems, floating into our yard, on the driveway a crisp carpet of bronze, on the hood of my car, under the wipers' thin blades. You have ripened, dried out, your leaves burnt to caramel corn. The fragrance all through the street. October. Pumpkins will soon lurk on the steps. Nothing's remembered for long. A pale fringe, jade-coloured now, already begins to feather your branches preparing for spring. Only robins and sparrows. Ceaseless. My niece died this time of year. *O, when the saints.* Three years ago. I can no longer conjure her sweet, smoky song.

four fifty p.m.
day ripens
to black

NIECE II: UNDER THE STARS WHAT A WONDERFUL WORLD

Your bark is the colour of barred owls, your circumference, its surface, sine waved as an owl's flight through firred forests, supple-winged, rivering, the owl's massive folding, unfolding through the tangle-twig maze. Your trunk is scalloped, muscled. I could take you to bed – kinky or comfort or all-night conversation. My sister's daughter died in her sleep in the season when the world disappears in bottomless night. In a hospital ward, not yet thirty-six. *What a Wonderful World*, she memorized every word. Her bravado, overflowing the depth of her wheelchair, ribbons a river, still with us now.

ice like jackknives
ruts winter streets
is this all there is?

THE LIGHT IN THIS DIURNAL

is oystergrey   cannot be so much seen as deduced wherever open-
ings in thickets of leaves permit a slip of cold sky   this light   almost enough
to discern   white as ash   white as the day before   and the day before that
this sub-light   five feet by four   mullioned in three standard panels   the sill
silted with fine off-white dust   studded with blue blown glass   red   yellow
a primary series to foil these unprismatic days

THE LIGHT IN THIS NOCTURNAL

at night the world bends though the sun has not so much as even appeared before its scheduled descent   the window opens into the street amber now with high-pressure sodium lamps   small winks inside shadowed leaves   opens out   an invitation   a film   the sky beyond is far far beyond must be believed   despite deficiencies of colour   so little evidence of sky from the only window on this floor that faces north   no stars for miles   no consolations

EVERYONE WANTS TO CHANGE THE WORLD BUT HOW MANY HELP THEIR NEIGHBOURS?

It is almost November and your leaves have fallen to ground. What's left are the pale downy bits along the fore-branches – I want to call them panicles but that's not their name – and the view through. The view through reveals the neighbour's white house caught in the crazy twists of your crown. The hydro pole like a sentinel stands still unflinching, guarding your corduroy trunk. Five wires fastened: hydro, telephone, thick as small wrists, high wires where birds keep the peace. Lines of power, lines of communication. Imbalance. Downtown, people are spreading their sleeping bags in alcoves for the night. Unlit. A man sleeps against the fence near the side of our house in the park. In the morning he folds his blankets, leaves as though he is leaving a quiet hotel. There are multiple barriers. There is the word *homeless*. Street people, neighbours. Fifty-six percent of the world's population live in its cities. Next year will be more. The vast, the remote, mutual isolations. The view through. The word *gratitude*. Every year, Katsura, you lose your sweet rounded leaves. Bodies grow older, people move from the countryside, cement hardens with age.

hummingbird
speed of ruby-red light –
talk about impermanence

WITH THEIR FLICKER-FORK TONGUES SNAKES TASTE THE BRIGHT BITTER AIR

After the downpour, O Katsura, fragrance swells round your trunk. Petrichor. Or pheromones. Your leaves' autumn blush, little cheeks. Night quickens too soon. Your leaves smell like pulled toffee, sweet, as if romance waits at the corner. These short days of Scorpio, snake eyes and ladders. I prefer summer, when darkness enters the heart only after long light spends the day. There is a villa in Kyoto that borrows your name. A house named after a tree. When my love whispers into my ear, she exhales candy kisses. When Māori greet one another in ceremony, they press foreheads and noses together, sharing the breath that comes straight from the gods. When she says I love you, she speaks from the earth's core.

two women together
alone
in the luminous house

NOVEMBER IS THE DAY AFTER HALLOWEEN

Day of the Dead   All Saints   freezes all calculation
last leaves on the hornbeam finally gather in heaps near the fence
the numbers descend by the minute
rain adds up to distraction

October's pumpkin caves into oblivion
November's backyard
all month the shell becomes a false face

WHEN PLACE IS A WINDOW

The upper floor is two windows:
one window south, fisheye over trees; one window boreal, doubled.
The horizon swells in frothings of grey.

Residing here not as a child nor as a mother nor
as a high-rise office worker in a city twenty years to the east
when other strictures applied.

The upper room overlooks this quarter world.
Parents walk children to daycare hand-in-forced-hand.
A dog leads its owner in mid-morning trance.
Every minute is change.

My eyes level this window – all there is
is this window.

This Street Is a Window

CONUNDRUM

erratic stones have fallen out of the sky
claims   promises   ecstatic time
which feet walked what range of soil
what lawyers said   say   what lawyers don't
layers of landfill
taken from the railway bed a few miles away
striated
clamshells   mussels   bones turned to sand
hooves click the pavement at night
small mammals whisper the grass
feathers scatter-heaps in the morning
almost inaudible to industrial ears

NOVEMBER BIRD COUNT FROM INSIDE THE HOUSE

Anna's hummingbird: one.
Back deck spread red for the indoor amaryllis.

Bald eagle: one.
Backyard, not tracking the hummer, cants east to the park.

House finch: zero.
House sparrow: zero.
Glaucous gull: zero (despite bucketing rain).

Spotted towhee: two.
Side yard from the basement window. One seen, one heard.

Golden-crowned kinglet: two.
Backyard, looping the giant cedar hedge.

American wigeon: zero.
Barn swallow: zero.
Canada goose: zero.
American robin: zero.

Blue-and-gold macaw: one.
Seen on a kitchen table two doors away.
Aged forty-nine.

American crow: seven, eight, no, nine. Wait, seventeen.
Across the street
dismantling the neighbour's new fence.

WHERE RAIN

December rains every day, blacktop buckled and mucked. I remain
despite rumours, earthquakes, kits, three days of water and pills,

despite three thousand miles from the Saint Lawrence River
where I grew up, farther still from the Clyde
where my father was born.

Impervious to threats of disaster, I remain,
having moved east to west as does the sun,
as crows fly at dawn.

The land that I live on is stolen, unceded as stars,
as crows scrolling sky.
Settler, drifter, colonial fault.

Because the land that I live on.
Incessant end-stops, caesuras, enjambments,

subversions of syntax. Not knowing
solutions. Borders, commas, and syntactical flaws,
caps, lower case. So much punctuation.

I live on the West Coast
far from the Big Apple.

Is it mistaken
to think that to write it, resolves? Syntax,
context, unceasing space.

I drift through old houses at night, conjure my mother.
What hubris.
Can writing this street ever.

I am grateful for people. Grateful for trees.

I float. My mother once papered the walls.
She remains. The rain
this December doesn't know how to stop.

PASSING THROUGH

the woman with unidentical twins not yet four months old
pushes the stroller through mornings with mist
short nights   dry coughs maybe flu   long days
umbrellas and cloth shopping bags   her three-year-old son
will follow her heels through the next year   and the next
one street then another   residential
this passage   existential   breakfast and dinner
pages of phone books no longer in use
as if proof

I lived until five on a street known as Sixth
not far from the aqueduct in mid-century Verdun
as if in a suburb of Rome

later I lived on a circle
called Green in Dorval   those days the street names
were English   I left at eighteen for a street numbered Fourth

once an apartment   bougainvillea scaling the carport
Protectorate Drive   Kenyatta's city   tail of a lion
the switch   swish   small twists of live paper
white bracts   magenta   tangerine
mauve and blood red

once a dead end near McGill

now I live on this street on the edge
on an island in the Pacific
where a mother strolls her three children
where a dog sniffs a blue box
stuffed with plastic and tins

all of us   citizens   old   young   mad
we are all passing through what passes through us
we have wings   we have leashes   delusions
grey tails and black Kevlar beaks

antlers   pink shoes   we wear backpacks   weave webs
swim sewers   we listen for wind
listen for sirens at three in the morning
fix cars   eyes   plant calla lilies   crocus bulbs in the fall
race across shingles   eat tulips
sit on porches and wave

IF A TREE MAKES A SOUND AND NOBODY HEARS

I am reading a book about trees   their hidden lives   the book suggests that
trees can feel pain   they cry when they're cut   limbs severed   sundered
it's winter   the rain has more or less stopped though I hear plaintive drips
drops   a car motor is running   near the sidewalk city workers have piled five
rounds of katsura wood   a pyramid stack   a neat sculptural installation on
the edge of my neighbour's soaked lawn   the rounds are more than fourteen
diametrical inches   from branches stout as trunks   one round bears a dark
scalloped line that snakes through the cross-section   a delicate yin-yang
sort of curve   a form of damage   possibly fungal   the city workers used an
automatic bucket lift   a chainsaw   there are power lines   the book says you
can hear a tree scream   their insides vibrate   they hum   these are slow worlds
these arboreals   the katsura is not native to this place   these boulevard trees
were imported more than twenty-five years ago   katsura live to be almost one
hundred years old even in this place where in summer their leaves curl almost
inside out with unbearable thirst   they heal   they endure even when harmed
last week city workers chainsawed the branches   I couldn't hear the tree cry
or even shout out   as I drove by I heard only the whine of the blade

fires burn in the hearth
how much
we don't know

TRUTH VS. TRUTH

this second-floor window that looks over the street scares me   a wasp tries
to get in tries to get out   the wasp itself doesn't scare me   but the wanting
to be somewhere else   though *scares* may not be the right word   maybe the
word is *disorients*   maybe I mean something like *confines   wearies*   maybe
the word is *entombs*

truth is the whole street frightens me   not so much its particulars   not the
man banned from the mall for importuning women cashiers   not the cars
their mishandled speed   not cracks in the sidewalks where trapped wrappers
wave as if wanting help   not teenagers slamming car doors in the night   no
but the whole business   this street   the idea of   landing in this particular
place late in life   staying put

truth is
maybe all streets

I was born on a street where all the buildings were joined at their sides

I raised my two children on five different streets in two separate cities
one a dead end   not all streets fester   not all streets spread dread in the
mid-afternoon   some lie long months under snow   snow in a street acts as a
buffer   the first street I lived on hung ice from the rails

Earle Street hangs cloud from branches and chimneys   some days the
cloud lifts

truth is most days the fear rolls off like a fog   an old habit   not just this street
this block   not just this house   this room   this window   my eyes   but still
sometimes an old enervation lays me out on my bed

BY DESIGN

Drops of rain cling with mathematical precision
along twigs with dark purple seeds,
small decorative crowns. Are they true seeds?
February: this is how days pass the time,
minute by minute. Promises,
small metaphors of hope. Although hope,
unlike raindrops,
is not what it was. We now know
hope comes skirmished with worry,
fractured longings, jackknives,
torches held high in the damp darkened air.

TEMPORALIA I

through the dawn
a rare snowfall
accumulations of slow-falling flakes
anomalous
onto the sidewalk in fat rounding inches,
floating onto the road,
into the laurel next door,
thick-mitted, white, this half-night, half-morning,
the shadows this side of the street lamp
in almost-dawning half-light
and the katsura
profuse now with new winter bulk
branches wrapped in white pelts,
ermine or the tails of Arctic fox,
otherworldly, quiescent,
nothing stirs,
these branches, burdened with
snow, hold up this new noiseless
day.

WHAT ELSE IS THERE TO FEAR

thrift shops   chaos   their leftover dust   the slow death of materiality
sickening

tainted food   slip-sliding creatures   spots that appear on the skin   dog
shit   goose shit   alarm clocks   black velvet art and people who disapprove
of black velvet art   carpenter ants in wordless procession   cockroaches in
toasters   voices loud on the street   canyoned streets   nights hollow as caves
torture   in any country anytime anykind anywhy

blackouts   the void   cancer   pain of the unending variety   scissors overly
sharp   fluids of the bodily kind   a street with water running in gutters
floods   the urgent rise of grey water

accidents involving cars planes buses   the body jammed up with
metal – Frida Kahlo – things that fall apart   vertigo

garbage loose on the street   sewage wet and the scum   plastic bags puffed up
like cumulus clouds   plastic bags in the ocean   plastic straws   being wrong
left out   falling straight-out-of-favour   falling   off ledges   did I mention ver-
tigo   dogs big as bears   packs of them   their sharpened teeth   sharp blades
cougars   grizzlies   snakes in my boots   earthquakes

high winds   kitchen fires   house fires   forest fires   the whole world
burning up

even so   though so much generates fear   there is still a certain uncertain cast
of the mind   flinching yes   but unflinching too

TEMPORALIA II

lopsides the bedroom   vaults   the milky way
sickens   skews   somersaults stars   spews
dwarf stars and white   thins   unsettles disputes
spins   its provenance completely unknown
unthreading my head   my feet
falling off in one gust

wheel within wheels
shapeless the room

these abstractions   nothing
of substance   neither dresser nor
walls as if each is a tumbler locked
into fear

gravity is in fact such a feeble force
nor is vertigo simply a word

IN CONSIDERATION OF THIS ONE GLOBAL WORLD

You are two parallel rows of boulevard trees. All related. Microbiologically interconnected. Seedlings together. Imported over three decades ago from Kyoto, Japan. You speak to each other in neither Latin nor Greek nor Japanese. But you speak. I imagine you sharing arboreal histories, global roots. Despite your relative youth, O Katsurae, I imagine you recall in your heartwood the earthquake of January 26, 1700. Seismic record: eighth day, twelfth month, twelfth year of the Genroku era when the wave struck the Japanese coast six hundred miles long though no one felt the ground shake. Nor had the wave a discernible origin. An orphan tsunami. I imagine you know the quake started here close to this street though no street was here at the time and no katsurae grew yet in this suburban subduction zone. I imagine you know that it left a ghost forest a grave a grove of western redcedars hanging high in the air turning silver becoming their own pillared tombs. Those venerable coniferous trees. The ground having plummeted from under their trunks that year on the banks of the Copalis River on the Washington coast to the south.

red sky morning
sparrows
fall

LIMINAL

five white-crowned sparrows
my wife reports
as she looks out dawn's bedroom window
no seven   no ten
curious I rise from my sick bed
to see the small rolling birds
move in and out of our bird's-eye glass view
darting under the viburnum's low branches
as though on miniature wheels
and out again
it's January or February
no
it's almost spring

YOUR PLACE ON THE GROUND IS NOT GUARANTEED

Even if vertigo, sewers rising to meet the street's curbs; even if whiplash, cork-screw, refusing to land, even if losing your mind, as if you finally go crazy. Even if. The tree remains, does not surrender its own vertical stance, even though its roots might be shallow. If houses peel from their moorings, sky collapsing to touch a black cat's soft breast, the tree will not follow the thrall of your mind. If dogs bay behind doors, if crows crash the nets of high-tension wires, if sirens sing the whole night, the tree holds. Steadfast. I ask you, how many trees does it take to keep us all sane? But you know the answer: more than exist.

evening sun lowers itself
grey squirrel
in full-body blush

OFFICE CHAIR AT A SMALL ATTIC WINDOW

brown asphalt tiles overlap row on row
perfect jigsaw
across the east side of the neighbour's low-sloping roof
where afternoons a grey squirrel races
pursued as we all are
by time
one way then back again
the squirrel switchbacks the roof's risky edge

I have seen this squirrel fly

I SEE UNCLEARLY AND YET

I try to see clearly. As if I might still be religious. I have no proper name for what it is that I do without benefit, or burden, of a single-point god. I try to be kind to the neighbour who will not allow his three-storey hedge to be trimmed despite the need of my five fledgling fruit trees for afternoon sun. I try to understand his point of view. Knowing so little. If I curse him, would I implode? Turn hypocrite, a metaphor, a meteor, a flash-frozen fish? Unlike astronauts, I am un-spaceshipped. Merely skinned. Knees. Palms. Chin. Wherever I have fallen before, I might fall again. Seeing so little, and yet.

dawn's glim
glaucous
the robin so bold

This Street Is a World

IN THE 4 A.M.

for my wife, Chris Fox

the chorusing rain so ravishing
we rush out of the house to make love
a before-dawn silvery love
the cupped radiance
streetlights bright as upswelling joy

the rain so glamorous we light up two cigarettes
our backs puddled in boulevard grass
under bare trees we study the miniature
teardrop chandeliers   blow collapsible smoke
into felled funnels of wet

the rain so clamorous
our breathing slows as though
we've started to live underground

in Montréal I wanted to make love on Mount Royal
wintertime   especially in winter   to climb the low slope
blankets in sacks for the snow
to press small warming dents under the boughs
my husband at the time declining the white invitation
though I asked more than once

but tonight   this soft fizzly falling   this rain insistent as pins
the contact unmistakable
murmurous   cool   the undertones
the universe falling
again and again

RAIN: RULES OF AFFECTION

At age ten, my grandson tells me
he loves the rain. He was born on this coast.
All the boys on his soccer team
love the rain too. His big brother
loves the rain. His neighbour's dog,
a short-haired collie, loves the rain,
refuses to walk in the sun.

On this West Coast rainforest street
the rain cascades almost every day,
quicksilvers the pavement, the trees.

I try. A new perspective: to love
what is more common to dread.

EARLY SPRING, THE KATSURA UNFOLDS THROUGH SLOW TIME

the violet-brown seed pods   little knots on each brownish-grey branch turn
into yellow-gold leaflets   become breeze   turn into Oregon juncos that turn
into rosy house finches   into early spring   March   small flecks of white
almost pink almost flowers   flowerets   dot the thin lower twigs   turn into
things-will-now-be-all-right   this time of year   expansive   and yet perpetual
in the rotation the violet-brown pods become thin-fingered ghosts

plum blossoms
unfurled umbrellas
praise the grey morning sky

ANYTHING APRIL

When April swells out of March,
it warns fools, first day,
before it turns cruel.
Beware false hope, nor weaken
in winter's protracted seclusion. This liminal cusp
can be suicidal.

And yet, mid-month turns again:
sun dogs and wings, green grasses bebirded.
Night constellations plumage the sky.

April advances on the backs of blue iris.
The street turns delirious. The viburnum
releases plumarian scents.

Anything happens: certain forms of reincarnation,
neighbours who died in the winter.
The thistle becomes the shape of true beauty.

NATURAL VS. NATURAL

I prefer neighbourhood walks   evening strolls
sidewalks where houses billow and bulge

to rambling at the ocean's rock edge
five minutes from home

I like the orange rectangular glow
that amplifies uncurtained windows
more than a sky blooming ultramarine   I like
the silhouettes of women moving through rooms
amber-lit at the end of the day
more than the stars

there are those
who consider this urban inclination unnatural
profane   as if humans in their own human lairs
are not natural too

METAPHOR II

being common does not protect the crow
from being hallmark cliché   unlike the junco or starling
nor from being the subject of outsized attention   romantic projection
fashion   the shape of the moment

as is the fox   this year
as is the moon   marked from the start as is
the ocean
the rose   bud   bloom   or faded
eyes too   blue sky   eagle   heart   even
lips and of course what we call love

what shape is common love   where
in a common heart

being common does not preclude
that though little is known
too much has already been said

(ROMANTIC) METAPHOR III:
VENERABLE BUT ALREADY DEAD

I fell my affection onto the place where you enter the earth, unbuckled and grassed. As if you are my true love. I know nothing about you except what I see, what is written. So insufficient. The purple finches are also in love, as are the flickers and chickadees who make their days in your crown. I have let you root in my heart, knowing nothing of yours. You survive in this city on this peopled street, grow year by year. How much you must miss the slopes of Japan, snow monkeys, the packs of wild dogs.

midsummer sun sets after nine
the rats
find the wall

(ROMANTIC) METAPHOR IV:
VENERABLE BUT COMMONLY FLORAL

Clouds of lilac outside my window, fanciful, their fragrance funereal. This is
how I arrange my devotion, imagined, these gestures freighted; the weight,
nineteenth-century. These worn-out adornments. I consign the mauve sprays
to your branches in my mind, pin them in place, an arboreal metamorphosis.
As for my wife, thirty-nine roses, one for each year, rococo, gathering
momentum. How can we not disturb the foundations with our extravagant
need? Displaced from the past, each metaphor fades, buried there too.

night is a river
a place
under the ribs

HOMELESSNESS: LIFE ON THE STREETS
IN THE PLURAL DIMENSION

whoever lives not on *a* street must live on
the streets   there is
    this particular difference
        singular versus the plural
    indefinite versus the definite article

how fixed the definition   how fixed the divide
there is
the urban core   shelters without shelter
streets without homes
commercial buildings   their doors   doorways
unused after five
except
for those on the street
unprotected
public spaces   their sleeping bags
second-hand   or third

GOOD FRIDAY: BLOSSOMS GIVE WAY

In the park a man in a bunny suit throws candy to children dressed in blue and gold-coloured jackets. The sun with us now. Later, the twins who live across the street are carried home, one in each parent's arms, the older child too. Under your new leaves, Katsura, an old man steers his bicycle into the road, a carry-cart hitched to the back, where his grandson sits under a canopy of bright yellow cloth. All the tortures archetypal, major and minor, happen in another place faraway long ago. Your leaves glisten sunbeams over the cart that carries the boy on his way home for his lunch.

northern flicker in a harris tweed suit
underskirts of red silk
perfectly one

HOW LONG IT TAKES TO BELONG TO THE EARTH

and wind for an eye
—May Swenson

I am only now
getting used
to this life   this
life   beginning now to settle in
it has been so many years

seeing
as I do even now
as through a window
but now the pane is no longer there
seeing
how the magnolia
its leaves flipping greenshine   their underside rust
in the wind
wide open
tree   light   mind

AFTER BREAKFAST COMES THE LIGHT

droplets spangle the mid-panel of my bedroom window
only the mid-panel   the rain shower that fast   precise

beyond the window   hydro wires bisect the maple   tips thin to red
beyond the maple   a quarter rainbow clichés the sky   the clichéd sky is blue

sun blinds   clears the sidewalk   saturates buds on the viburnum
cars shine chrome   doors yellow   a man leaves his house in green trousers

the street washes itself in detail   almost too much to bear
the clarity   the hopefulness of it all

white trim partitions one house from another
to say the street below approximates perfection

is to engage the imperfect   to say
the line of rooftops reaches out towards infinity

is to pin the eye to the horizon
a white dog at the end of a purple leash

a boy in a pink hat   the desire for the original
might be the original sin   wanting all things new again   but

who can help it   who refuses paradise
when light comes after sudden rain

TEMPORALIA III

The orange cat that safeguarded the street from behind its living-room window.
No longer.
All things, they say, arise, run amuck, run to ground.
They drove away in the silver pickup they bought two years before.
Waving, passing each house, driving west down the street.
Gone. For good.
Or for worse. Beginning all over again.
Infinitesimal deaths, the exquisite hiatus of loss.
They emptied their garage onto the base of the katsura close to the sidewalk.
Everything free. Take it. Take it.
A short-legged chair, dowels, picture frames with no glass.
A wicker basket big enough for three litters of rats.
A tie rack, a park bench, a mirror, its glass crazed.
Four lamps without shades.
Last year the family with non-identical twins returned to the north.
I rescued the chair.
It squats in my basement, high-backed, an oversized toad painted black.
No one sits in it.
The two women who owned the guard cat split up.
One moved to the mainland.
But the wicker basket, yes. With no rats.
Four years ago, a water main geysered onto the street.
The optometrist moved to Mount Doug, taking his eye charts
and golden retriever.
A five-month-old baby moved into the former rental directly across.
The young boy two doors away became a young man who now
works in meats.
Three neighbours died. One at a time.
Trees continue to spread, lift their branches up over the houses.
The effort it takes in the morning.
Each year proliferates shade.
The story of the dog poisoned for digging up tulips;
no longer. No one tells that story anymore.
Public spaces, notions of time, the way the street.

Things beginning. And then.
All things. And then.
My mother visits mainly at night.
On an irregular basis; she's been dead thirty-five years.
Sometimes now she un-dyes her hair.

Notes

Several poems in this collection have been previously published: "Come the Ungulate" in *The Malahat Review* and in *Best Canadian Poetry*; "Blue Moon Enters the Street from the South East" and "In the 4 A.M." in *The Maynard* and *Canadian Literature / Littérature canadienne*; "In Japanese the Word for This Tree Is *Katsura*" and "In Consideration of This One Global World" in *Haiku Canada Review*; "This Street Is / Is Not a River" in Betsy Warland's Oscar's Salon; "After Breakfast Comes the Light" first appeared in my poetry collection, *He Leaves His Face in the Funeral Car*, published by Caitlin Press. Many thanks to them all.

Thanks to Elaine Weidner, neighbour and block watch co-captain, who gave me permission to use her emails to create a number of found poems.

The term *temporalia* was borrowed from David W. McFadden's "Stimulation Galore," in *What's the Score* (Mansfield Press, 2012).

"Come the Ungulate" was inspired by Steve Collis's "Come the Revolution," in *To the Barricades* (Talonbooks, 2013).

"Urban Geography I" was taken from Michel de Certeau's *The Practice of Everyday Life*, third edition, trans. Steven F. Rendall (University of California Press, 2011).

"Urban Geography II" was taken from Jonathan Murdoch's *Post-Structuralist Geography: A Guide to Relational Space* (Sage Publishing, 2005).

"Urban Geography III" was taken from Harold Carter's *The Study of Urban Geography*, fourth edition (Hodder Arnold, 1995).

"If a Tree Makes a Sound and Nobody Hears" draws on Peter Wohlleben's *The Hidden Life of Trees: What They Feel, How They Communicate—Discoveries from a Secret World* (Greystone Books, 2016).

Acknowledgments

Many thanks to the BC Arts Council for acknowledging the value of my work through their financial support. Thanks also to the members of my two writing groups (Patricia Young, Julie Paul, Cynthia Woodman Kerkham, Christine Walde, Barbara Lampard, Yvonne Blomer, Isa Milman, Beth Kope, Terry Ann Carter, Sue Gee, Barbara Herringer) for reading a number of the poems that appear in this collection, and for their useful suggestions. Special thanks to Terry Ann Carter, who so generously taught me the elements of the haibun. Thanks to my friend, Yaana Dancer, who introduced me to *The Practice of Everyday Life* and *The Study of Urban Geography*. Huge gratitude to Catriona Strang, who edited this collection both thoroughly and thoughtfully. Thanks to my kind neighbours who have been enthusiastic about this collection. Finally, I must acknowledge my deep appreciation for the many valuable contributions of my wife, first reader, and professional in-house editor, Chris Fox, who lives with me on Earle Street. I am so lucky for all of you in my writing life.

Arleen Paré is a Victoria writer. She has published five collections of poetry, two of which are cross-genre. She has been short-listed for the BC Book Prizes Dorothy Livesay Poetry Award, and has won a Golden Crown Award for Lesbian Poetry, the City of Victoria Butler Book Prize, and a Governor General's Literary Award.

Photo by Chris Fox